A LITTLE SPOONFUL OF CHICKEN SOUP FOR THE SOUL® JUST FOR FRIENDS

Photo by Jade Albert/FPG
Design by Kim Hokanson

ISBN 1-58375-436-9
Printed in Mexico

A
Little
Spoonful of

Chicken
Soup
for the Soul®
Just for Friends

Best Friends Forever

When I said good-bye to my best friend, Opal, we promised to write and vowed that we'd see each other again. At fourteen, our futures seemed full of possibilities, despite our coming separation. It was June 1957, and we had spent two and a half of the happiest years of our lives on Chitose Air Force base in Japan. Now her family was being transferred to England, mine to Florida. What hurt most about leaving each other was that she was not only my first, but my best friend.

Growing up with a father in the military meant moving often. The two-room schoolhouse on the northern island of Kikkaido was my ninth school—and I was only in sixth grade when I arrived. Opal's roving childhood was similar to mine, except that I was terribly, horribly, painfully, miserably shy. I loathed always being "the new girl." Once or twice I'd managed to make a friend, but before we could get to know each other well, I'd moved on to a different school.

Then one January day in 1955, I stood in the doorway of my newest classroom. As always, my stomach ached with dread, and shivers of fear ran through me like tiny sharp arrows. I hoped no one could tell I was trying to hold back tears. Twenty kids silently stared at me, and I turned red from my ears down to my toes. I kept my eyes on the floor, sneaking only quick peeks at the strange faces. Then I saw a girl beaming, her smile like warm sunshine flooding my shaking soul. She actually seemed to welcome me! When the teacher told me to take the desk next to Opal's, some of my frozen terror began to melt slightly.

"Hi, I'm Opal." Her voice carried the twang of the Midwest, her face was round, her eyes soft behind her thick glasses, her hair long and brown. And as I quickly learned, her heart was crafted of twenty-four karat gold.

That first day, as we moved from history to math to English, she helped me find the right place in the books and filled me in on the other kids.

Because we had fourth, fifth and sixth grades in the same room, the teacher would take small groups up front while the rest of us worked at our desks, very much like the school in *Little House on the Prairie*. With only five of us in sixth grade, the angels were working overtime when they made sure one of them was Opal.

By the end of that first day, an unspoken promise had been made. Opal and I knew we would be best friends, the first either of us had found. During the next months, more and more new kids moved

to the base and Opal welcomed
everyone, teaching me by example
to do the same. Red-haired Maureen
arrived and became an especially
close friend. But we all hung out
together, both boys and girls, playing
kickball and Red Rover, skiing on the
snowy mound behind my house,
exploring the woods where we were
officially forbidden to go, swimming
in the frigid pool when the short
summers arrived, camping on what

we hoped was an extinct volcano, attending the Japanese Cherry Blossom and Snow festivals.

In that large group, Opal and I were rock-solid best friends, a true Mutt and Jeff duo. She was tall and slim, I was short and plump; she was good in math, I loved reading; she wasn't athletic, but cheerfully joined the games and sports I dragged her into. Her father was a master sergeant (the fire chief! So romantic!), mine a lieutenant colonel. She admired my get-up-and-go; I admired her gentleness with young children, the way she always gave of herself, her ability to see the smallest rose in a thicket of thorns. Our differences meshed and never clashed.

Two years flew by—miracle years filled with fun and growth and discovery. Then the rumors began. The Air Force was closing the base, and we would all be transferred back to the States that summer, headed for different assignments, hundreds or thousands of miles apart.

As promised, Opal and I wrote occasional letters (on military salaries, long distance phone calls were out of the question) until we were sixteen. I was in boarding school when her last letter came. She'd fallen in love with an older man—nineteen—an airman first class. She'd left her family in England and returned to the States to marry him. She had just given birth to a beautiful baby girl.

I wrote back right away but didn't get an answer. Knowing how Opal found writing an awful chore, I wrote again and again. Finally my letters were returned: forwarding address unknown. How I worried about her! To be married and have a baby at sixteen! I knew her so well: I knew she'd be a wonderful mother, but I also knew she was too young to be married.

I graduated from boarding school and then college, was married, had three babies, divorced, remarried. My children grew up, went to college, and my daughter was now a mother. So often I thought of Opal, wondering where she was, if she was all right, if she was happy. I'd talk about our blissful years together, and my family knew all about my best friend.

One sweaty hot August day in 1991 the telephone rang. "Is this Louise?"

"Yes."

"Is this Louise Ladd from Japan?"

"Who are you?" I roared.

"This is Opal."

Dancing around and jumping up and down, I shouted out my joy.

Thirty-four years after we said good-bye, she had found me. Sorting through piles of stuff after a recent move, she had opened an ancient box marked "papers." My letter from 1959 was in it. Immediately she called everyone named Ladd who lived anywhere near my old address in Maryland; then, refusing to give up, she called my boarding school. After much begging and pleading, the alumnae office finally gave her my phone number.

That Christmas, Opal and her second husband drove from

Omaha, Nebraska, to spend a few days with us in Connecticut. She looked exactly the same. She sounded exactly the same. She radiated the same warmth and love I'd always known. She'd missed me as much as I'd missed her. She managed to find the good in life. Twenty-four karat gold does not tarnish.

And now we are together again: best friends, forever.

—Louise Ladd
A 5th Portion of Chicken Soup for the Soul

On Friendship

Friends are there to heal the wounds
To pull you out of saddened tunes
To brighten up your cloudy skies
To clear up fictitious lies

Friends are there with open arms
To comfort you and block the harms
To keep your secrets hidden away
To entertain you when you want to play

Friends are there, smile or tear
Friends are there, happiness or fear
Friends are fun and friends are clever
And the ties that bind friends will
   last forever.

— Harmony Davis, age 14
   Chicken Soup for the Kid's Soul

It takes a lot of understanding, time and trust to gain a close friendship with someone. As I approach a time of my life of complete uncertainty, my friends are my most precious asset.

ERYNN MILLER, AGE 18

A Simple Christmas Card

Abbie, shy and reserved, started ninth grade in the big-city high school in the center of town. It never occurred to her that she would be lonely. But soon she found herself dreaming of her old eighth-grade class. It had been small and friendly. This new school was much too cold and unfriendly.

No one at this school seemed to care if Abbie felt welcome or not. She was a very caring person, but her shyness interfered with making friends. Oh, she had those occasional buddies, you know, the kind that took advantage of her kindness by cheating off her.

She walked the halls every day almost invisible; no one spoke to her, so her voice was never heard. It reached the point where she believed that her thoughts weren't good enough to be heard. So she continued to stay quiet, almost mute.

Her parents were very worried about her, for they feared she'd never make friends. And since they were divorced, she probably needed to talk with a friend very badly. Her parents tried everything they could to help her fit in. They bought her the clothes and the CDs, but it still didn't work.

Unfortunately, Abbie's parents didn't know Abbie was thinking of ending her life. She often cried herself to sleep, believing that no one would ever love her enough to be her real friend.

Her new pal Tammy used her to do her homework by pretending to need help. Even worse, Tammy was leaving Abbie out of the fun she was having. This only pushed Abbie closer to the edge.

Things worsened over the summer; Abbie was all alone with nothing to do but let her mind run wild. She let herself believe that this was all that life was cracked up to be. From Abbie's point of view, it wasn't worth living.

She started the tenth grade and joined a Christian youth group at a local church, hoping to make friends. She met people who on the outside seemed to welcome her, but on the inside wished she'd stay out of their group.

By Christmas time Abbie was

so upset that she was taking sleeping pills to help her sleep. It seemed as though she was slipping away from the world.

Finally, she decided that she would jump off the local bridge on Christmas Eve, while her parents were at a party. As she left her warm house for the long walk to the bridge, she decided to leave her parents a note in the mailbox. When she pulled down the door to the mailbox, she found letters already there.

She pulled the letters out to see who they were from. There was one from Grandma and Grandpa Knight, a couple from the neighbors... and then she saw one addressed to her. She tore it open. It was a card from one of the guys in the youth group.

Dear Abbie,

I want to apologize for not talking with you sooner, but my parents are in the middle of a divorce, so I didn't have a chance to talk with anyone. I was hoping you could help me with some questions I have about divorced kids. I think we could become friends and help each other. See you at Youth Group on Sunday!

Sincerely your friend,
Wesley Hill

She stared at the card for a while, reading it over and over again. "Become friends," she smiled, realizing that someone cared about her life and wanted plain, quiet Abbie Knight as a friend. She felt so special.

She turned around and went back to her house. As soon as she

walked in the door, she called Wesley.
I guess you could say he was a
Christmas miracle, because friendship
is the best gift you can give anyone.

— Theresa Peterson
  Chicken Soup for the Teenage Soul

My New Best Friend

Today I met a great new friend
Who knew me right away
It was funny how she understood
All I had to say

She listened to my problems
She listened to my dreams
We talked about love and life
She'd been there, too, it seems

I never once felt judged by her
She knew just how I felt
She seemed to just accept me
And all the problems I'd been dealt

She didn't interrupt me
Or need to have her say
She just listened very patiently
And didn't go away

I wanted her to understand
How much this meant to me
But as I went to hug her
Something startled me

I put my arms in front of me
And went to pull her nearer
And realized that my new best friend
Was nothing but a mirror.

— Retold by Kimberly Kirberger
   Chicken Soup for the Teenage Soul

Seeing, Really Seeing

His nose was all smooshed looking, like maybe his mom had dropped him when he was a baby. His ears were two, maybe even two-and-a-half, sizes too big for his head. And his eyes! His eyes bulged like they were ready to pop right out of their sockets. His clothes were nice, Tim had to admit. But he was still the homeliest kid he'd ever seen.

So why was the new kid

leaning on Jennifer Lawrence's locker like they were best friends or something? She was a cheerleader and one of the coolest girls in school. And why was she smiling at him instead of twisting her nose all funny like she did when she looked at Tim? *Strange*, he thought. *Really strange*.

By lunchtime, Tim had forgotten about the new kid. He sat down at his usual table in the corner, all alone. Tim was a loner. He wasn't

as ugly as the new kid, just a little
on the heavy side and kind of nerdy.
Nobody talked to Tim much, but he
was used to it. He had adjusted.

About halfway through his
peanut butter and ketchup sandwich,
Tim looked up and saw that kid again.
He was holding his lunch tray and
standing over Jennifer, grinning like
he'd just aced a math test. And she
was grinning, too. Then she moved
over and made room on the bench

next to her. *Strange. Really strange.*

But even stranger was what the new kid did. Tim would have plunked into that seat so fast, his lunch bag would have been left behind, just hanging in the air. But not this new kid. He shook his head, looked around and walked straight to Tim's table.

"Mind if I join you?" he asked.

Just like that. *Mind if I join you? Like the entire eighth grade was fighting to sit at my table or something*, Tim thought.

"Sure," said Tim. "I mean no. I don't mind."

So the kid sat down. And he came back, day after day, until they were friends. Real friends.

Tim had never had a real friend before, but Jeff—that was his name— invited Tim to his house, on trips with his family and even hiking.

Funny thing was…one day Tim

realized he wasn't so heavy anymore. *All that hiking, I guess*, thought Tim. And kids were talking to him, nodding to him in the hallways, and even asking him questions about assignments and things. And Tim was talking back to them. He wasn't a loner anymore.

One day, when Jeff sat down at the table, Tim had to ask him. "Why did you sit with me that first day? Didn't Jen ask you to sit with her?"

"Sure, she asked. But she

didn't need me."

"Need you?"

"You did."

"I did?"

Tim hoped nobody was listening. *This was a really dumb conversation*, he thought.

"You were sitting all alone," Jeff explained. "You looked lonely and scared."

"Scared?"

"Uh huh, scared. I knew that

look. I used to have one, too, just like it."

Tim couldn't believe it.

"Maybe you didn't notice, but I'm not exactly the best-looking guy in school," Jeff went on. "At my old school I sat alone. I was afraid to look up and see if anyone was laughing at me."

"You?" Tim knew he sounded stupid, but he couldn't picture Jeff by himself. He was so outgoing.

"Me. It took a friend to help me see that I wasn't alone because of my nose or my ears. I was alone because I never smiled or took an interest in other people. I was so concerned about myself that I never paid attention to anyone else. That's why I sat with you. To let you know someone cared. Jennifer already knew."

"Oh, she knows, all right," Tim said as he watched two guys fighting to sit near her. Tim and

Jeff both laughed. It felt good to laugh and I've been doing a lot of it lately, realized Tim.

Then Tim looked at Jeff. Really looked. *He isn't so bad looking,* thought Tim. *Oh, not handsome or anything like that. But he isn't homely. Jeff is my friend.* That's when Tim realized that he was seeing Jeff for the first time. Months earlier all he had seen was a funny-looking nose

and "Dumbo" ears. Now he was
seeing Jeff, really seeing him.

— Marie P. McDougal
    Chicken Soup for the Kid's Soul

My Friend Anthony

Whenever I think back to third grade, I think of my friend Anthony. He had blond hair and big, brown, expressive eyes. I had been surprised to see that he was in my class because he was older than I was.

Although Anthony had AIDS and knew his days were limited, he was always eager to come to school and try to lead a normal life. Some days, he got tired and had to leave early. His mother usually came every day to eat lunch with him or just to be with him. It seemed like he always had a positive outlook on things even though he knew everything wasn't okay. He came to school with what appeared to be a medicine pouch attached to his waist. Many times I felt sorry for him because I knew he must have been in pain.

In June of that year, Anthony died. After that, I sometimes lay awake at night, afraid to go to sleep because I was afraid of dying.

I knew Anthony had left his body to go to a better place, a place without pain, but I felt bad for his family because they would always feel empty without Anthony.

During the year that I had gone to school with Anthony, I had grown to respect him and his mother, too. Through her love and compassion, she taught Anthony, as well as others such as myself, to be brave, and to love, care for and respect everyone. Anthony had taught me to live life to the fullest, and I intend to do just that.

— Katie Short, age 12
  Chicken Soup for the Kid's Soul

Friendships multiply joys
and divide grief.

THOMAS FULLER

Edna Mae:
Lesson in Prejudice

Edna Mae was one of my best friends when I was in the first grade. When it came time for her birthday party, all the girls in the class were invited. Each day in school there was great excitement.

"What kind of cake you gonna have?" we'd ask.

"Are you gonna have games with prizes? And decorations? Birthday hats?"

Edna Mae would just smile and shake her head. "Wait and see," she'd say. Together we counted down the days until Saturday, the date on the invitation.

Finally the day arrived. I wrapped my gift, put on my best party dress and waited what seemed like hours for my mother to say, "Time to go!"

I was glad that I was the first

to arrive because I got to help place the candy cups all around—one for each of the twelve guests. The table was covered with a special "Happy Birthday" tablecloth with matching plates and cups. Balloons were everywhere. Streamers crisscrossed the ceiling in the hallway, the living room and especially the dining room, where the table was all set. It looked like a fairyland.

"Oh, Edna Mae! Oh, Edna Mae!" was all I could say.

Edna Mae's mom sent us out to the front porch to wait for the other girls. Edna Mae lived on the edge of town, and most of the other girls had never been to her house before.

"Some might be having trouble finding us," her mother said.

We sat down on the steps and

waited and waited and waited. Edna
Mae began to cry. I felt so awful that
I didn't know what to say. Finally
her mother came out and announced,
"Let the party begin!" She ushered
us into the house, tied a blindfold
around our eyes, put a tail with a
pin in our hands and led us to the
donkey taped on the wall.

"Whoever gets the tail closest
to the right place wins the first super

prize!" she said. My tail ended up near the donkey's nose. Edna Mae's tipped the right front hoof. We laughed and laughed.

Together, Edna Mae and I played all the games and shared all the prizes. We even got to eat two pieces of cake each.

On the way home, I asked my mother, "Why didn't the other girls come? Edna Mae felt so bad."

My mother hesitated and then said sadly, "Honey, the others didn't come because Edna Mae is black."

"She's not black," I protested. "She just looks like she has a tan all year long."

"I know, honey. But Edna Mae is not like any of the other girls in the class, and some folks are afraid of those who are different from them. People are prejudiced, honey. That's what adults call it: prejudice."

"Well, those girls are mean. They made Edna Mae cry. I'm never gonna be prejudiced!" I said.

My mother put her arm around me and said, "I'm glad, honey. And I'm glad that Edna Mae has a good friend like you."

— Sandra Warren
Chicken Soup for the Kid's Soul